This
Weekly 2020
PLANNER
Belongs To

_____

2020 Holiday Schedule

Date	Holiday
Wednesday, January 1	New Year's Day
Monday, January 20	Birthday of Martin Luther King, Jr.
Monday, February 17	Washington's Birthday
Monday, May 25	Memorial Day
Friday, July 3	Independence Day
Monday, September 7	Labor Day
Monday, October 12	Columbus Day
Wednesday, November 11	Veterans Day
Thursday, November 26	Thanksgiving Day
Friday, December 25	Christmas Day

2020

JANUARY 2020

m	tu	w	th	f	sa	su
		1	2	3	4	5
6	7	8	9	10	11	12
13	14	15	16	17	18	19
20	21	22	23	24	25	26
27	28	29	30	31		

FEBRUARY 2020

m	tu	w	th	f	sa	su
					1	2
3	4	5	6	7	8	9
10	11	12	13	14	15	16
17	18	19	20	21	22	23
24	25	26	27	28	29	

MARCH 2020

m	tu	w	th	f	sa	su
						1
2	3	4	5	6	7	8
9	10	11	12	13	14	15
16	17	18	19	20	21	22
23	24	25	26	27	28	29
30	31					

APRIL 2020

m	tu	w	th	f	sa	su
		1	2	3	4	5
6	7	8	9	10	11	12
13	14	15	16	17	18	19
20	21	22	23	24	25	26
27	28	29	30			

MAY 2020

m	tu	w	th	f	sa	su
				1	2	3
4	5	6	7	8	9	10
11	12	13	14	15	16	17
18	19	20	21	22	23	24
25	26	27	28	29	30	31

JUNE 2020

m	tu	w	th	f	sa	su
1	2	3	4	5	6	7
8	9	10	11	12	13	14
15	16	17	18	19	20	21
22	23	24	25	26	27	28
29	30					

JULY 2020

m	tu	w	th	f	sa	su
		1	2	3	4	5
6	7	8	9	10	11	12
13	14	15	16	17	18	19
20	21	22	23	24	25	26
27	28	29	30	31		

AUGUST 2020

m	tu	w	th	f	sa	su
					1	2
3	4	5	6	7	8	9
10	11	12	13	14	15	16
17	18	19	20	21	22	23
24	25	26	27	28	29	30
31						

SEPTEMBER 2020

m	tu	w	th	f	sa	su
	1	2	3	4	5	6
7	8	9	10	11	12	13
14	15	16	17	18	19	20
21	22	23	24	25	26	27
28	29	30				

OCTOBER 2020

m	tu	w	th	f	sa	su
			1	2	3	4
5	6	7	8	9	10	11
12	13	14	15	16	17	18
19	20	21	22	23	24	25
26	27	28	29	30	31	

NOVEMBER 2020

m	tu	w	th	f	sa	su
						1
2	3	4	5	6	7	8
9	10	11	12	13	14	15
16	17	18	19	20	21	22
23	24	25	26	27	28	29
30						

DECEMBER 2020

m	tu	w	th	f	sa	su
	1	2	3	4	5	6
7	8	9	10	11	12	13
14	15	16	17	18	19	20
21	22	23	24	25	26	27
28	29	30	31			

BIRTHDAYS

January	February	March

April	May	June

BIRTHDAYS

July   August   September

October   November   December

Mon 30	
Tue 31	
Wed 1	
Thu 2	

Fri

3

Sat

4

Sun

5

Notes

Mon 6	

Tue 7	

Wed 8	

Thu 9	

Fri

10

Sat

11

Sun

12

Notes

Mon	
13	

Tue	
14	

Wed	
15	

Thu	
16	

Fri

17

Sat

18

Sun

19

Notes

Mon	
20	
Tue	
21	
Wed	
22	
Thu	
23	

Fri

24

Sat

25

Sun

26

Notes

Mon
27

Tue
28

Wed
29

Thu
30

Fri

31

Sat

1

Sun

2

Notes

February   2020

Mon 3	
Tue 4	
Wed 5	
Thu 6	

Fri

7

Sat

8

Sun

9

Notes

Mon	
10	

Tue	
11	

Wed	
12	

Thu	
13	

	Fri
	14

	Sat
	15

	Sun
	16

Notes

Mon	
17	
Tue	
18	
Wed	
19	
Thu	
20	

Fri

21

Sat

22

Sun

23

Notes

Mon	
24	

Tue	
25	

Wed	
26	

Thu	
27	

	Fri
	28

	Sat
	29

	Sun
	1

Notes

Mon 2	
Tue 3	
Wed 4	
Thu 5	

Fri

6

Sat

7

Sun

8

Notes

Mon 9	
Tue 10	
Wed 11	
Thu 12	

	Fri
	13

	Sat
	14

	Sun
	15

Notes

Mon 16	
Tue 17	
Wed 18	
Thu 19	

Fri

20

Sat

21

Sun

22

Notes

Mon	
23	

Tue	
24	

Wed	
25	

Thu	
26	

Fri

27

Sat

28

Sun

29

Notes

Mon	
30	

Tue	
31	

Wed	
1	

Thu	
2	

	Fri
	3

	Sat
	4

	Sun
	5

Notes

Mon	
6	

Tue	
7	

Wed	
8	

Thu	
9	

Fri

10

Sat

11

Sun

12

Notes

Mon	
13	

Tue	
14	

Wed	
15	

Thu	
16	

Fri

17

Sat

18

Sun

19

Notes

Mon 20	
Tue 21	
Wed 22	
Thu 23	

Fri

24

Sat

25

Sun

26

Notes

Mon 27	
Tue 28	
Wed 29	
Thu 30	

| | Fri |
| | 1 |

| | Sat |
| | 2 |

| | Sun |
| | 3 |

Notes

Mon	
4	

Tue	
5	

Wed	
6	

Thu	
7	

	Fri
	8

	Sat
	9

	Sun
	10

Notes

Mon	
11	

Tue	
12	

Wed	
13	

Thu	
14	

2020 May

Fri

15

Sat

16

Sun

17

Notes

Mon	
18	

Tue	
19	

Wed	
20	

Thu	
21	

	Fri
	22

	Sat
	23

	Sun
	24

Notes

Mon	
25	

Tue	
26	

Wed	
27	

Thu	
28	

Fri

29

Sat

30

Sun

31

Notes

Mon	
1	

Tue	
2	

Wed	
3	

Thu	
4	

Fri

5

Sat

6

Sun

7

Notes

Mon	
8	

Tue	
9	

Wed	
10	

Thu	
11	

| | Fri |
| | 12 |

| | Sat |
| | 13 |

| | Sun |
| | 14 |

Notes

Mon	
15	

Tue	
16	

Wed	
17	

Thu	
18	

Fri

19

Sat

20

Sun

21

Notes

Mon	
22	
Tue	
23	
Wed	
24	
Thu	
25	

Fri

26

Sat

27

Sun

28

Notes

Mon	
29	

Tue	
30	

Wed	
1	

Thu	
2	

Fri

3

Sat

4

Sun

5

Notes

Mon	
6	

Tue	
7	

Wed	
8	

Thu	
9	

Fri

10

Sat

11

Sun

12

Notes

Mon	
13	
Tue	
14	
Wed	
15	
Thu	
16	

Fri

17

Sat

18

Sun

19

Notes

Mon 20	
Tue 21	
Wed 22	
Thu 23	

Fri

24

Sat

25

Sun

26

Notes

Mon 27	
Tue 28	
Wed 29	
Thu 30	

	Fri
	31

	Sat
	1

	Sun
	2

Notes

Mon	
3	

Tue	
4	

Wed	
5	

Thu	
6	

Fri

7

Sat

8

Sun

9

Notes

Mon 10	
Tue 11	
Wed 12	
Thu 13	

Fri

14

Sat

15

Sun

16

Notes

Mon	
17	
Tue	
18	
Wed	
19	
Thu	
20	

Fri

21

Sat

22

Sun

23

Notes

Mon 24	
Tue 25	
Wed 26	
Thu 27	

| | Fri |
| | 28 |

| | Sat |
| | 29 |

| | Sun |
| | 30 |

Notes

Mon 31	
Tue 1	
Wed 2	
Thu 3	

2020

September

Fri

4

Sat

5

Sun

6

Notes

Mon	
7	

Tue	
8	

Wed	
9	

Thu	
10	

Fri

11

Sat

12

Sun

13

Notes

Mon	
14	

Tue	
15	

Wed	
16	

Thu	
17	

2020

September

Fri

18

Sat

19

Sun

20

Notes

Mon	
21	

Tue	
22	

Wed	
23	

Thu	
24	

Fri

25

Sat

26

Sun

27

Notes

Mon	
28	

Tue	
29	

Wed	
30	

Thu	
1	

Fri

2

Sat

3

Sun

4

Notes

Mon 5	
Tue 6	
Wed 7	
Thu 8	

Fri

9

Sat

10

Sun

11

Notes

October   2020

Mon	
12	
Tue	
13	
Wed	
14	
Thu	
15	

Fri

16

Sat

17

Sun

18

Notes

October   2020

Mon 19	
Tue 20	
Wed 21	
Thu 22	

Fri

23

Sat

24

Sun

25

Notes

Mon 26	
Tue 27	
Wed 28	
Thu 29	

Fri

30

Sat

31

Sun

1

Notes

Mon	
2	

Tue	
3	

Wed	
4	

Thu	
5	

Fri

6

Sat

7

Sun

8

Notes

Mon	
9	

Tue	
10	

Wed	
11	

Thu	
12	

Fri

13

Sat

14

Sun

15

Notes

Mon 16	
Tue 17	
Wed 18	
Thu 19	

2020

November

Fri

20

Sat

21

Sun

22

Notes

Mon	
23	

Tue	
24	

Wed	
25	

Thu	
26	

Fri

27

Sat

28

Sun

29

Notes

Mon	
30	

Tue	
1	

Wed	
2	

Thu	
3	

2020

December

Fri

4

Sat

5

Sun

6

Notes

December   2020

Mon	
7	
Tue	
8	
Wed	
9	
Thu	
10	

Fri

11

Sat

12

Sun

13

Notes

Mon 14	

Tue 15	

Wed 16	

Thu 17	

Fri

18

Sat

19

Sun

20

Notes

Mon 21	
Tue 22	
Wed 23	
Thu 24	

Fri

25

Sat

26

Sun

27

Notes

December 2020

Mon	
28	
Tue	
29	
Wed	
30	
Thu	
31	

Fri

1

Sat

2

Sun

3

Notes

2021 AT A GLANCE

JANUARY

M	T	W	T	F	S	S
28	29	30	31	1	2	3
4	5	6	7	8	9	10
11	12	13	14	15	16	17
18	19	20	21	22	23	24
25	26	27	28	29	30	31
1	2	3	4	5	6	7

FEBRUARY

M	T	W	T	F	S	S
1	2	3	4	5	6	7
8	9	10	11	12	13	14
15	16	17	18	19	20	21
22	23	24	25	26	27	28
1	2	3	4	5	6	7
8	9	10	11	12	13	14

MARCH

M	T	W	T	F	S	S
1	2	3	4	5	6	7
8	9	10	11	12	13	14
15	16	17	18	19	20	21
22	23	24	25	26	27	28
29	30	31	1	2	3	4
5	6	7	8	9	10	11

APRIL

M	T	W	T	F	S	S
29	30	31	1	2	3	4
5	6	7	8	9	10	11
12	13	14	15	16	17	18
19	20	21	22	23	24	25
26	27	28	29	30	1	2
3	4	5	6	7	8	9

MAY

M	T	W	T	F	S	S
26	27	28	29	30	1	2
3	4	5	6	7	8	9
10	11	12	13	14	15	16
17	18	19	20	21	22	23
24	25	26	27	28	29	30
31	1	2	3	4	5	6

JUNE

M	T	W	T	F	S	S
31	1	2	3	4	5	6
7	8	9	10	11	12	13
14	15	16	17	18	19	20
21	22	23	24	25	26	27
28	29	30	1	2	3	4
5	6	7	8	9	10	11

NOTES:

2021 AT A GLANCE

JULY

M	T	W	T	F	S	S
			1	2	3	4
5	6	7	8	9	10	11
12	13	14	15	16	17	18
19	20	21	22	23	24	25
26	27	28	29	30	31	

AUGUST

M	T	W	T	F	S	S
						1
2	3	4	5	6	7	8
9	10	11	12	13	14	15
16	17	18	19	20	21	22
23	24	25	26	27	28	29
30	31					

SEPTEMBER

M	T	W	T	F	S	S
		1	2	3	4	5
6	7	8	9	10	11	12
13	14	15	16	17	18	19
20	21	22	23	24	25	26
27	28	29	30			

OCTOBER

M	T	W	T	F	S	S
				1	2	3
4	5	6	7	8	9	10
11	12	13	14	15	16	17
18	19	20	21	22	23	24
25	26	27	28	29	30	31

NOVEMBER

M	T	W	T	F	S	S
1	2	3	4	5	6	7
8	9	10	11	12	13	14
15	16	17	18	19	20	21
22	23	24	25	26	27	28
29	30					

DECEMBER

M	T	W	T	F	S	S
		1	2	3	4	5
6	7	8	9	10	11	12
13	14	15	16	17	18	19
20	21	22	23	24	25	26
27	28	29	30	31		

NOTES:

Made in the USA
Monee, IL
14 December 2021

85446588R00069